THE WILLIE LYNCH LETTER:
THE MAKING OF A SLAVE

William Lynch
Introduction and Edition:
Lattoya Cybele Williams
IAP © 2020

Las Vegas: IAP, 2020.

admin@iappublishing.com

IAP © 2020.

All rights reserved.

Printed in the United States

Main Cover Image: *The Power of Music*, 1847, by William Sidney Mount, an American 19th century daily life painter. The image was selected because it seems the black man is listening to a very serious conversation the white people are having. He is in fact listening to music. Sometimes something is not what it seems to be. The other paintings showing people playing banjo, bones, and violin are also by W. S. Mount.

Lynch, Willie; Williams, Lattoya Cybele.

The Willie Lynch Letter: The Making of a Slave

1. History.   2. American History

The paper used in this publication meets the minimum requirements of the American National Standard for Information Sciences-Permanence of Paper for Printed Library Materials, ANSI Z39.48-1992.

Contents

Introduction   5

The Willie Lynch Letter   19

Let's Make a Slave   23

Introduction

When the Willie Lynch letter was first published in 1993 in Internet, it was accepted by most people as an authentic and enlightening piece of revelation about how farmers treated black slaves in the 1700s. Anne Taylor, a researcher in the University's Thomas Jefferson Research Center, had found the Lynch speech in a local newspaper, the St. Louis Black Pages, and posted it on a website maintained by the University of Missouri-St. Louis. When it was first published on the net, the letter caused a huge impact at the time, typically on black people.

Two years later, Louis Farrakhan addressed the multitudes in October 1995 at the Million Man March quoting key passages from Lynch's narrative to illustrate the vestiges of slavery:

> "We as a people now have been fractured, divided and destroyed, filled with fear, distrust and envy," Farrakhan said. "Therefore, because of fear, envy and distrust of one another, many of us as leaders, teachers, educators, pastors and persons are still under the control mechanism of our former slave masters and their children."

Lynch teaches "I use fear, distrust and envy for control."[1] So this is where these words used by Farrakhan in his speech came from.

Since the 1990s, once the letter has been published, it was included as authentic in books addressing the black-white relation in history, such as *Legacy* by Horace Cheeves and Denise N. Cheeves, the self-published *The Illusion of Civilization* by Jermaine Jackson, *Thinking with the Big Head* by Jamil Aaron, who attributes *Let's Make a Slave* to F. Douglass, and many others. Its impact on black people was huge.

What Farrakhan and many others didn't know is that the letter is most probably an absolute 20th century forgery. Here are a few of many reasons the letter is fake:

1. Style: Nobody in the early 1700s would have written in the style the letter was written. This is typically an end-of-20th century style, it is not even from the first years of the 20th century. In fact, this seems to be a style of someone who is alive today. Another incredible aspect in my view is that there are just a very few spelling issues in the whole text, which is uncommon for someone writing a letter about three hundred years ago, when people could write without uniformity in the same letter as the literacy level wasn't high in general. It seems this text was well written in a computer using a spell-checker. Based on the

---

[1] P. 18 here, in the paragraph beginning with "gentlemen".

style I would state this text was definitively written between 1960 and 1990. The text could also have been edited by the publisher when it was published in the newspaper in the 1970s though.

2. Literacy: In 1702 Virginia, less than 50% of the local people were literate, if we can call them literate, as public schools were not available in colonial Virginia. The literate people typically had only a few years of learning at school or at home. The numbers were much lower in rural areas. So why should a small farmer write a well-written letter for other farmers if possibly some of them couldn't even read it well? Moreover, someone who had a "modest plantation" in West Indies in 1702 was most probably an illiterate and definitively couldn't write such letter or even create such reasoning presented in the letter.

3. The impossible course: Small farmers at that time, such as this owner of a "modest plantation", seldom had more than five enslaved people so I ask myself how could a three or four slave farmer in West Indies be invited to teach the richest farmers in Virginia who owned hundreds of slaves about the right way of keeping slaves? Just imagine a small businessman today with four or five employees invited from a small country abroad maybe in the Bahamas to teach the biggest businessmen in the United States. Would that happen? Nope.

It doesn't make sense. Even if a small farmer found out the right way of keeping slaves, would a big and rich farmer be interested in listening what a small one had to say? And why would he teach them, for money? The author is naïve and even pretentious, as he says the Roman Empire would love his fantastic method.

4. Place: The writer presents himself as Lynch, a small farmer living abroad. This is very convenient, as it would be easier to recognize this as a forgery if his name could be found in local records.

5. Slave literacy: Slaves were largely illiterate and systematically prohibited from formally learning the language as a means of social control. The section about the language control is anachronistic. A sentence such as "For example, if you take a slave, if you teach him all about your language, he will know all your secrets" doesn't make much sense as no farmer would teach English well to any slave (also because he didn't know it well enough to teach and) because it was against the law. Except for a few cases, nobody was doing that at that time, so no need to say "I will teach you the secret way of dealing with slaves: Don't teach them English." It's true that not teaching English created a language barrier and the slaves would find harder to organize and revolt, but at the same time some knowledge of English was necessary anyway for basic communication, typically for the enslaved

house workers. Many slaves learned to read through Christian instruction, but only those whose (Christian) owners allowed. After 1831, the prohibition to teach slaves was extended in some states even to free Blacks. Slave owners saw slave literacy as a threat so no need for the teaching: don't teach them English. Nobody did.

6. Slavery existed before America was discovered: The farmer teaches: "For example, if you told a slave that he must perform in getting out 'our crops' and he knows the language well, he would know that 'our crops' didn't mean 'our crops' and the slavery system would break down." Then it seems for me, for the same reason capitalism would break down... Most of the slaves who were to the Americas were already slaves in Africa or were born in America as slaves, so they had the notion of working for someone else "tribe" as in bonded labor or slavery or the notion they were in the slavery condition since they were able to understand some words. Probably any African man knew that if their tribe or nation lost a war to another African tribe or nation at a certain moment in his life, he would be killed or captured and his status would be changed into a slave for the winners (who could later trade them) and he would be slave forever or until finding a way to escape. This was the general culture in Africa and the African gods allowed slavery so that the African kings allowed it too. So the expression in the title "making a slave" is

against African history, because most of the men were told probably when they were young that they could become a slave someday in Africa or they were born slaves in America. Women and children were always turned into slaves if a war was lost – when captured. They could be later traded as slaves one, two or three times until they arrived at the coast in Africa and crossed the Ocean knowing they were slaves, except young boys, because they had been captured (typically by black hunters) and traded (once or more) as a slave until they reached a port in Africa where they would see a white man for the first time in their lives. And they would be typically be very frightened as they found white men ugly or found they were into witchery because of their sailing ships. It's important to know that black slavery existed because, it existed since Ancient times in Rome and Greece and in Africa.

7. Connotation. The farmer makes consistent reference to "slaves" — which is possible, though it is more likely people would refer to people in bondage simply as "negroes." In the first paragraph, he states that "Ancient Rome would envy us if my program is implemented," but the word "program" did not enter the English language with this connotation until 1837 and became widely used with such meaning in the 20th century. Concerning the terms "indoctrination" and "self-refueling", the first

word didn't carry it current connotation until 1832; the second didn't even enter the language until 1811 and some say even later. "Fool proof", for example, was not in use until the early 20th century. The farmer also uses the word "Black," with an upper-case "B," to describe African Americans, which began to be used as a common ethnic identifier in the 20th century. So based on the connotation of these words, this letter was certainly written in the 20th century. No other possibility exists.

8. Lamb or lion? The attribution of forgeries to people who never lived or lived centuries ago is not uncommon in history, typically when the original text was handwritten and could easily be created or changed. The forger's goal is to manipulate people, leading them to take an active or passive position related to powerful people or politics. More than once in the past documentation was forged to make people act as a lamb, accepting their leaders and everything they impose, or a lion, not accepting their leaders or situation. Concerning W. Lynch forgery, it was forged to make people act as a lion against the white people, as *The Protocols of the Elders of Zion* was, to put German people against the Jews and other forgeries or fake statements were made in the 1930s in Germany by the Nazi leaders against the Jews. The opposite soft power model is very common in Christianity and other religions, which were

typically manipulated by emperors, kings, and pharaohs, for example, in fake miracles and prophecies stories attributed to saints, bishops, gods etc. Some scholars even state that the biblical life of Christ is a forgery created about 1900 years ago by the Roman Empire or the fist Christians, attributing to Jesus Christ amazing miracles he never really did. Forgeries will be found in ancient Eastern religions too, not only in Western ones. Antiquity was a time when the political leaders created gods, religions, cults, and beliefs to manipulate the people. But forgeries continued to be made in Middle Ages and in the last centuries.

9. Lack of historical records: There is no record of William Lynch in the beginning of the 1700s in the Virginia Historical Society and nowhere else. Moreover, there is no track of the original 18th century manuscript or publication either and not even a 19th century publication. Unless the original source is found and considered authentic by experts, this composition will be always considered a forgery by scholars.

In fact, over the years, Anne Taylor, the one who first published the letter online, came to the conclusion that the speech was fake – a view shared by most of the historians today. She said the style sounded too American and too modern, and "the use of the language during those days was closer to Elizabethan English in its construct and spelling."

When Howard Denson, the publisher of the St. Louis Black Pages, was called in the 1990s and asked about the authenticity of this letter he published himself, he said:

> "I don't know, and frankly, I don't give a damn. I've done a lot of things that I thought would have a lot of appeal. This appeared in one of the ugliest layouts we've ever done. But I've never run a piece that got the response this one got. There's something truly magical about it. Don't ask me to explain it."

Appeal, to get a response, something magical... are expressions he used to justify the authenticity. As the letter impressed and still impresses people, even when they know it's fake, the letter reached a certain level of historical importance anyway from the historical viewpoint.

Some versions of the letter have introductions attached, such as a foreword attributed to Frederick Douglass, or citations falsely attributing Lynch's name as the source of the word "lynching". For example:

"This speech was delivered by Willie Lynch on the bank of the James River in the colony of Virginia in 1712. Lynch was a British slave owner in the West Indies. He was invited to the colony of Virginia in 1712 to teach his methods to slave owners there. The term "lynching" is derived from his last name. "

While there is disagreement about the origins of the word lynch — some associate it with Charles Lynch, and others to another William Lynch who lived at the end of the 1700s, both judges — certainly it didn't come from 1712 W. Lynch as lynching appears in the literature in the 1800s. It most probably derived from one of these two judges, who lived later.

The other important 20th century forgery sometimes connected to the letter is the Frederick Douglass introduction about the letter. The introduction is basically an extraction of paragraphs from books written by F. Douglass, originally without reference to the letter, used to address the letter. In this case, Douglass really wrote these words, but did not intend to relate them to the W. Lynch letter:

"To the slave-owners of Virginia

The following treatise, to the knowledgeable, will be the missing link[2] that has been sought to explain how we were put into the condition that we find ourselves in today. It confirms the fact that the slaveholder tried to leave nothing to chance when it came to his property; his slaves. It demonstrates, how out of necessity, the slave holder had to derive a system for perpetuating his cash crop, the slave, while at the same time insulating himself from retribution by his unique property.

A careful analysis of the following 'handbook', will hopefully change the ignorant among our people who say 'Why study slavery?' Those narrow minded people will be shown that the condition of our people is due to a scientific and psychological blue print[3] for the perpetuation of the mental condition that allowed slavery to flourish. The slaveholder was keenly aware of the breeding principles of his livestock and the following treatise demonstrated that he thoroughly used those principles on his human live stock as well, the African Slave, and added a debilitating

---
[2] The expression. "missing link", first attested in 1851, was not widely used in the 19th century, when Douglass lived.
[3] Even though blueprint was first used in 1842, "psychological blueprint" seems to be a 20th century expression.

psychological component as well.

It was the interest and business of slaveholders to study human nature, and the slave nature in particular, with a view to practical results, and many of them attained astonishing proficiency in this direction. They had to deal not with earth, wood and stone, but with men and by every regard they had for their own safety and prosperity they needed to know the material on which they were to work.[4]

Conscious of the injustice and wrong they were every hour perpetrating and knowing what they themselves would do, were they the victims of such wrongs, they were constantly looking for the first signs of the dreaded retribution. They watched, therefore, with skilled and practiced eyes, and learned to read, with great accuracy, the state of mind and heart of the slave, through his stable face. Unusual sobriety, apparent abstraction, sullenness, and indifference, indeed any mood out of the common way afforded ground for suspicion and inquiry.[5]

---

[4] This paragraph was written by Frederick Douglass, but it was extracted from *My Bondage and My Freedom*, first published in 1855, and inserted here as falsely related and connected to the W. Lynch letter. (pp 286-287)

[5] The first part of this paragraph, from "conscious" to "inquiry" was also written by Douglass, but extracted from *Life and Times of Frederick Douglass*, originally published in 1892. (pp 195-196). The last words (let's make...) were falsely included, attributed to F. Douglass. This tactic used by the forger of this document here is a typical one used in Middle Ages when forgeries in

'Let's Make a Slave' is a study of the scientific process of man breaking and slave making. It describes the rationale and results of the Anglo Saxon's ideas and methods of insuring the master/slave relationship."

As you can see from the footnotes, the composition is based on words written by Douglass, but all the references to the letter are fake and were inserted by the forger, who extracted some authentic words from Douglass' books.

Lattoya Cybele Williams

Historian

---

manuscripts were produced: part of the text was really written by the person, but the other part mixed to it was composed by the forger to tell a message only the forger want to send, using the famous person name, in this case F. Douglass.

The Willie Lynch Letter

December 25, 1712[6]

Gentlemen:

I greet you here on the bank of the James River in the year of our Lord one thousand seven hundred and twelve. First, I shall thank you, the gentlemen of the Colony of Virginia, for bringing me here. I am here to help you solve some of your problems with slaves. Your invitation reached me on my modest plantation in the West Indies, where I have experimented with some of the newest and still the oldest methods for control of slaves. Ancient Rome's would envy us if my program is implemented.

As our boat sailed south on the James River, named for our illustrious King, whose version of the Bible we cherish, I saw enough to know that your problem is not unique. While Rome used cords of wood as crosses for standing human bodies along its highways in great numbers, you are here using

---

[6] The Christmas day is chosen probably to cause impact on the Christian readers. Why a speech on a day when a modest farmer as W. Lynch should be with his family?

the tree and the rope on occasions. I caught the whiff of a dead slave hanging from a tree, a couple miles back. You are not only losing valuable stock by hangings, you are having uprisings, slaves are running away, your crops are sometimes left in the fields too long for maximum profit, You suffer occasional fires, your animals are killed.

Gentlemen, you know what your problems are; I do not need to elaborate. I am not here to enumerate your problems, I am here to introduce you to a method of solving them. In my bag here, I have a foolproof method for controlling your black slaves. I guarantee every one of you that if installed correctly it will control the slaves for at least 300 years. My method is simple. Any member of your family or your overseer can use it. I have outlined a number of differences among the slaves and make the differences bigger. I use fear, distrust and envy for control.

These methods have worked on my modest plantation in the West Indies and it will work throughout the South. Take this simple little list of differences and think about them. On top of my list is "age" but it's there only because it starts with an "A." The second is "COLOR" or shade, there is intelligence, size, sex, size of plantations and status on plantations, attitude of owners, whether the slaves live in the valley, on a hill, East, West, North, South, have fine hair, course hair, or is tall or short. Now that you have a list of differences, I shall give you an outline of action, but before that, I shall assure you that distrust is stronger than trust and envy stronger than adulation, respect or admiration. The Black slaves after receiving this indoctrination shall carry on and will become self-refueling and self-generating for hundreds of years, maybe thousands. Don't forget you must pitch the old black Male vs. the young black Male, and the young black Male against the old black male. You must use the dark skin slaves vs. the light skin slaves, and the light skin slaves vs. the dark skin slaves. You must use the female vs. the male. And the male vs. the female. You must also have you white servants and overseers distrust all Blacks. It is necessary that your slaves trust and depend on us. They must love, respect and trust only us. Gentlemen, these kits are your keys to control. Use them. Have your wives and children use them, never miss an opportunity. If used intensely for one year, the slaves themselves will remain perpetually distrustful of each other.

Thank you gentlemen

Let's Make a Slave

It was the interest and business of slave holders to study human nature, and the slave nature in particular, with a view to practical results. I and many of them attained astonishing proficiency in this direction. They had to deal not with earth, wood and stone, but with men and by every regard they had for their own safety and prosperity they needed to know the material on which they were to work. Conscious of the injustice and wrong they were every hour perpetuating and knowing what they themselves would do. Were they the victims of such wrongs? They were constantly looking for the first signs of the dreaded retribution. They watched, therefore with skilled and practiced eyes, and learned to read with great accuracy, the state of mind and heart of the slave, through his sable face. Unusual sobriety, apparent abstractions, sullenness and indifference indeed, any mood out of the common was afforded ground for suspicion and inquiry. [7]

Let us make a slave. What do we need? First of all we need a black nigger man, a pregnant nigger woman and her baby nigger boy. Second, we will

---

[7] Paragraph extracted from *Life and Times of Frederick Douglass*, originally published in 1892, p. 195-196

use the same basic principle that we use in breaking a horse, combined with some more sustaining factors. What we do with horses is that we break them from one form of life to another that is we reduce them from their natural state in nature. Whereas nature provides them with the natural capacity to take care of their offspring, we break that natural string of independence from them and thereby create a dependency status, so that we may be able to get from them useful production for our business and pleasure.

Cardinal Principles for Making a Negro

For fear that our future Generations may not understand the principles of breaking both of the beast together, the nigger and the horse. We understand that short range planning economics results in periodic economic chaos; so that to avoid turmoil in the economy, it requires us to have breath and depth in long range comprehensive planning, articulating both skill sharp perceptions. We lay down the following principles for long range comprehensive economic planning. Both horse and niggers is no good to the economy in the wild or natural state. Both must be broken and tied together for orderly production. For orderly future, special and particular attention must be paid to the female and the youngest offspring. Both must be crossbred to produce a variety and division of labor. Both must be taught to respond to a peculiar new language. Psychological and physical instruction of containment must be created for both. We hold the six cardinal principles as truth to be self-evident, based upon the following the discourse concerning the economics of breaking and tying the horse and the nigger together, all inclusive of the six principles laid down about. NOTE: Neither principle alone will suffice for good economics. All principles must be employed for orderly good of the nation. Accordingly, both a wild horse and a wild or nature nigger is dangerous even if captured, for they will have the tendency to seek their customary freedom, and in doing so, might kill you in your sleep. You cannot rest. They sleep while you are awake, and are awake while you are asleep. They are dangerous near the family house and it requires too much labor to watch them away from the house. Above all, you cannot get them to work in this natural state. Hence both the horse and the nigger must be broken; that is breaking them from one form of mental life to another. Keep the body take the mind! In other words break the will to resist. Now the breaking process is the same for both the horse and the nigger, only slightly varying in degrees.

But as we said before, there is an art in long range economic planning. You must keep your eye and thoughts on the female and the offspring of the horse and the nigger. A brief discourse in offspring development will shed light on the key to sound economic principles. Pay little attention to the generation of original breaking, but concentrate on future generations.

Therefore, if you break the female mother, she will break the offspring in its early years of development and when the offspring is old enough to work, she will deliver it up to you, for her normal female protective tendencies will have been lost in the original breaking process. For example take the case of the wild stud horse, a female horse and an already infant horse and compare the breaking process with two captured nigger males in their natural state, a pregnant nigger woman with her infant offspring. Take the stud horse, break him for limited containment.

Completely break the female horse until she becomes very gentle, whereas you or anybody can ride her in her comfort. Breed the mare and the stud until you have the desired offspring. Then you can turn the stud to freedom until you need him again. Train the female horse where by she will eat out of your hand, and she will in turn train the infant horse to eat out of your hand also. When it comes to breaking the uncivilized nigger, use the same process, but vary the degree and step up the pressure, so as to do a complete reversal of the mind. Take the meanest and most restless nigger, strip him of his clothes in front of the remaining male niggers, the female, and the nigger infant, tar and feather him, tie each leg to a different horse faced in opposite directions, set him a fire and beat both horses to pull him apart in front of the remaining nigger. The next step is to take a bull whip and beat the remaining nigger male to the point of death, in front of the female and the infant. Don't kill him, but put the fear of God in him, for he can be useful for future breeding.

The Breaking Process of the African Woman

Take the female and run a series of tests on her to see if she will submit to your desires willingly. Test her in every way, because she is the most important factor for good economics. If she shows any sign of resistance in submitting completely to your will, do not hesitate to use the bull whip on her to extract that last bit of resistance out of her. Take care not to kill her, for in doing so, you spoil good economic. When in complete submission, she will train her offspring in the early years to submit to labor when he becomes of age. Understanding is the best thing. Therefore, we shall go deeper into this area of the subject matter concerning what we have produced here in this breaking process of the female nigger. We have reversed the relationship in her natural uncivilized state she would have a strong dependency on the uncivilized nigger male, and she would have a limited protective tendency toward her independent male offspring and would raise male off springs to be dependent like her. Nature had provided for this type of balance. We reversed nature by burning and pulling a civilized nigger apart and bull whipping the other to the point of death, all in her presence. By her being left alone, unprotected, with the male image destroyed, the ordeal caused her to move from her psychological dependent state to a frozen independent state. In this frozen psychological state of independence, she will raise her male and female offspring in reversed roles.

For fear of the young males life she will psychologically train him to be mentally weak and dependent, but physically strong. Because she has become psychologically independent, she will train her female off springs to be psychological independent. What have you got? You've got the nigger women out front and the nigger man behind and scared. This is a perfect situation of sound sleep and economic. Before the breaking process, we had to be alertly on guard at all times.

Now we can sleep soundly, for out of frozen fear his woman stands guard for us. He cannot get past her early slave molding process. He is a good tool, now ready to be tied to the horse at a tender age. By the time a nigger boy reaches the age of sixteen, he is soundly broken in and ready for a long life of sound and efficient work and the reproduction of a unit of good labor force. Continually through the breaking of uncivilized savage nigger, by throwing the nigger female savage into a frozen psychological state of independence, by killing of the protective male image, and by creating a submissive dependent mind of the nigger male slave, we have created an orbiting cycle that turns on its own axis forever, unless a phenomenon occurs and re shifts the position of the male and female slaves. We show what we mean by example. Take the case of the two economic slave units and examine them closely.

The Nigger Marriage

We breed two nigger males with two nigger females. Then we take the nigger males away from them and keep them moving and working. Say one nigger female bears a nigger female and the other bears a nigger male. Both nigger females being without influence of the nigger male image, frozen with an independent psychology, will raise their offspring into reverse positions. The one with the female offspring will teach her to be like herself, independent and negotiable (we negotiate with her, through her, by her, we negotiate her at will). The one with the nigger male offspring, she being frozen with a subconscious fear for his life, will raise him to be mentally dependent and weak, but physically strong, in other words, body over mind. Now in a few years when these two offspring's become fertile for early reproduction we will mate and breed them and continue the cycle. That is good, sound, and long range comprehensive planning.

Warning: Possible Interloping Negatives

Earlier we talked about the non-economic good of the horse and the nigger in their wild or natural state; we talked out the principle of breaking and tying them together for orderly production. Furthermore, we talked about paying particular attention to the female savage and her offspring for orderly future planning, then more recently we stated that, by reversing the positions of the male and female savages, we created an orbiting cycle that turns on its own axis forever unless a phenomenon occurred and resift and positions of the male and female savages. Our experts warned us about the possibility of this phenomenon occurring, for they say that the mind has a strong drive to correct and re-correct itself over a period of time if I can touch some substantial original historical base, and they advised us that the best way to deal with the phenomenon is to shave off the brute's mental history and create a multiplicity of phenomena of illusions, so that each illusion will twirl in its own orbit, something similar to floating balls in a vacuum.

This creation of multiplicity of phenomena of illusions entails the principle of crossbreeding the nigger and the horse as we stated above, the purpose of which is to create a diversified division of labor thereby creating different levels of labor and different values of illusion at each connecting level of labor. The results of which is the severance of the points of original beginnings for each sphere illusion. Since we feel that the subject matter may get more complicated as we proceed in laying down our economic plan concerning the purpose, reason and effect of crossbreeding horses and nigger, we shall lay down the following definition terms for future generations.

Orbiting cycle means a thing turning in a given path. Axis means upon which or around which a body turns. Phenomenon means something beyond ordinary conception and inspires awe and wonder. Multiplicity means a great number. Sphere means a globe. Cross breeding a horse means taking a horse and breeding it with an ass and you get a dumb backward ass long headed mule that is not reproductive nor productive by itself.

Crossbreeding niggers mean taking so many drops of good white blood and putting them into as many nigger women as possible, varying the drops by the various tone that you want, and then letting them breed with each other until another cycle of color appears as you desire. What this means is this; Put the niggers and the horse in a breeding pot, mix some assess and some good white blood and what do you get? You got a multiplicity of colors of ass backward, unusual niggers, running, tied to a backward ass long headed mule, the one productive of itself, the other sterile. (The one constant, the other dying, we keep the nigger constant for we may replace the mules for another tool) both mule and nigger tied to each other, neither knowing where the other came from and neither productive for itself, nor without each other.

Control the Language

Crossbreeding completed, for further severance from their original beginning, we must completely annihilate the mother tongue of both the new nigger and the new mule and institute a new language that involves the new life's work of both. You know language is a peculiar institution. It leads to the heart of a people. The more a foreigner knows about the language of another country the more he is able to move through all levels of that society. Therefore, if the foreigner is an enemy of the country, to the extent that he knows the body of the language, to that extent is the country vulnerable to attack or invasion of a foreign culture. For example, if you take a slave, if you teach him all about your language, he will know all your secrets, and he is then no more a slave, for you can't fool him any longer. For example, if you told a slave that he must perform in getting out "our crops" and he knows the language well, he would know that "our crops" didn't mean "our crops" and the slavery system would break down, for he would relate on the basis of what "our crops" really meant. So you have to be careful in setting up the new language for the slaves would soon be in your house, talking to you "man to man" and that is death to our economic system. In addition, the definitions of words or terms are only a minute part of the process. Values are created and transported by communication through the body of the language. A total society has many interconnected value system. All the values in the society have bridges of language to connect them for orderly working in the society. But for these language bridges, these many value systems would sharply clash and cause internal strife or civil war, the degree of the conflict being determined by the magnitude of the issues or relative opposing strength in whatever form.

For example, if you put a slave in a hog pen and train him to live there and incorporate in him to value it as a way of life completely, the biggest problem you would have out of him is that he would worry you about provisions to keep the hog pen clean, or the same hog pen and make a slip and incorporate something in his language where by he comes to value a house more than he does his hog pen, you got a problem. He will soon be in your house.

www.ingramcontent.com/pod-product-compliance
Lightning Source LLC
Chambersburg PA
CBHW021916160426
42813CB00096B/127